THIS BOOK BELONGS TO

_____

A NOTE TO PARENTS

This series of Really Cool is on Faith. It helps to create an awareness for children on the importance of faith in God, rather than faith in their own ability.

The Bible makes it clear that we are only able to do all things through Christ that strengthens us. Philippians 4:13

James thought he could rely on his abilities and knowledge but later found out he needed to trust God.

Children can easily trust someone especially when they know the person is reliable. Tell them how reliable God is, tell them how you have trusted God in the past and He gave you success.

This is a good opportunity to tell them about Jesus who is always there to help them in life's challenges.

Key Focus: Faith in God, simply put as "Trust God in all things"

by
Lauretta Amata Olowu

James spent the evening in his room practicing his times table for his maths test. The next day, he was excited to tell his parents how prepared he was for his test.

"Mum! I am ready for my maths test," James said excitedly.

"I have practiced my times table and know it well."

"Wow! That's great son, I am really proud of you," said Mum.

"I know you have read and are well prepared for the test, but it's best to put your trust in God to help you remember all you have read," Mum said.

"Mum are you saying that God can make me remember anything if I forget it?" asked James.

"Yes," Mum replied.

"James I want you to know that there's nothing God cannot do if we ask Him in faith," Mum added.

"Mum! do you mean anything?" asked James.

"Yes son, anything," Mum answered. James was surprise at what his mum had said.

"Do you mean God can do anything?" He asked again.

"Yes son, God can do all things, everything, and anything if we ask Him in faith," said Mum.

As Dad walked in James said,

"Dad, Mum said God can do anything and all things if I ask in faith. That's really cool!"

"Yes James, Mum is right. You will find it in Luke chapter one verse thirty-seven." Dad replied.

"Wow! that's really cool." James said.

"Let's pray," said Dad. "Dear God as James goes to school to write his test, please help him to remember all he has read in Jesus name."

"Amen!" Mum and James responded.

"Bye son, all the best in your test. I love you," said Mum.

As James' dad walked James to school, James kept thinking of the conversation he had with his parents. He didn't think that he would need to apply faith by trusting and depending on God during his maths test.

James looked at the board and did the first five questions but was stuck on the last one.

"Oh no, I can't remember what 6x9 is and I read it yesterday," James whispered to himself.

"I wish Dad was here, so I could ask him to remind me."

James struggled to remember what the answer to the 6x9 is, but he couldn't figure it out.

James whispered again to himself.

"Emm......,6x9"

"Wait a minute," James said to himself.
"Dad said God can do anything if I ask Him in faith."

James prayed in silence.

"Dear God, my parents said you can do anything if I ask in faith. Please God, remind me what 6x9 is. I read it yesterday but can't remember it right now. Thank you God for bringing it back to my memory. In Jesus name, Amen."

"What is 6x9, James asked himself again?" Immediately, he had an idea to multiply 6x10 and take away 6.

"James said 6x10=60 and 60-6=54. Oh yes I remember, 6x9 is 54!

"Thank you God. You are a superstar, who can do all things.
Faith is really cool." Woohoo, James exclaimed.

As James and his dad went home, he told his dad what had happened to him during his maths test and how he had to put his trust in God for the answer.

"Wow!" said his Dad. "I told you that God can do all things."

"Yes Dad, I believe now that God can do all things." Said James.

"FAITH is really COOL." James added.

"Mum! Guess what? You're right. God can do all things, He helped me figure out the answer to the last question in my maths test. FAITH is really COOL!" James said excitedly.

"That's great, I told you God can do all things, Mum responded with a smile."

James' mum read the book of Matthew from the bible to James and explained it to him. She drew his attention to chapter seven, verse nine to eleven.

Letting him know that if parents could give their children what they asked for, then God that made both parents and children will surely give both children and parents anything they ask Him for in FAITH.

Matthew chapter seven verse seven says, "ask and you will recieve, seek and you will find, knock and the door will be open to you."

As James slept, he dreamt of what his Mum had read to him from the bible in the book of Matthew chapter seven, verse nine to eleven.

"You parents—if your children ask for a loaf of bread, do you give them a stone instead?

Or if they ask for a fish, do you give them a snake? Of course not! So if you sinful people know how to give good gifts to your children, how much more will your heavenly Father give good gifts to those who ask him".

PRAYER

Dear children, to have the right to pray to God and recieve answer. You must accept the free gift of His son (Jesus), by believing that Jesus came and died for your sin and by accepting Him as your Lord and saviour.

Say this simple prayer, "Lord Jesus, I believe you can do all things. I believe you can save me from my sin. I give you my heart, come and be my Lord and my saviour in Jesus name, Amen."

SCRIPTURES ON FAITH

BOOK	CHAPTER	VERSE
HEBREWS	11	6
HEBREWS	11	1
MARK	9	23
MARK	11	23,24
LUKE	1	37
ROMANS	10	17
2CORINTHIANS	5	7
MATTHEW	7	9-11
JAMES	2	26

ACTIVITIES

Read Proverbs 10:7 and fill in the gap.
The .... of the righteous is ....

Read Luke 1:37 and fill in the gap.
For with God .... shall be ....

James was excited to tell his parents about what?
....

Fill in the gap. Tips on page 21.
.... said his Dad........... is really ....

Explain what faith in God means?
....

TESTIMONIAL

Pastor Lauretta has combined her pastoral and parental grace in presenting bible teaching in a simple but exceptionally pictorial manner that every child would read, reason and respond to as a 'really cool faith'. I commend the book to parents to acquire for their children. It is truly cool!

Olalekan Akinleye, FCCA
Parish Pastor, RCCG (The Lord's Sanctuary, London)

Lauretta Olowu's Really Cool book series on Faith, is a gift to have by all parents for their children and useful for Sunday Schools too. Really Cool on Faith is a pictorial book written to help children understand what God can do for them if they trust Him.

Thank you for the simplicity in which you wrote the book in order to catch the reader's heart on how to believe God for practical daily living. It is very encouraging and for someone like me, it is faith made simple to understand.

Pastor Lola Oyebade
Senior Pastor HOTRIC (London)

This story is a simple but amazing way to show how God is interested in everything that concerns us. With this book faith has been put in the simplest form for the young ones to understand.

As a childcare provider myself and a parent, I think children will draw strength and courage from knowing that they have a friend they can trust in God.

Esther Brown
Nursery Manager (Graceland Day Nursery, London)

I love that you have used "Faith is Really Cool" as the topic. That is a wonderful concept for children and as an adult, I really enjoyed reading this book.

Susanna Wright
Staff Pastor, Holy Trinity Hounslow (London)
Author of "A Dairy of Private Prayer" By John Baillie. Updated and Revised by Susanna Wright

www.ingramcontent.com/pod-product-compliance
Lightning Source LLC
Chambersburg PA
CBHW061818290426
44110CB00026B/2904